BEDS

BEDS

Wade Stevenson

The McCall Publishing Company

NEW YORK

To Nivola, without whose work,
and
To Cynthia, without whose absences and presences
my beds could not have been made.

CONTENTS

BEDS

What Is in the Bed? ॐ

What is in the bed?
There is sand, there is water.
There is stone and bricks of sun,
a simple, natural life.
There is a river
that will answer every desire
you have if you will only lean
over and look into it long enough.
There are sunflowers and horses
calm, cool valleys and pillows
and nude bodies baked brown into loaves
by the suns of multiple midnights.
There are trees as simple
and sincere as violins,
women with breasts as bright as arabesques,
fluffy, white slabs of clouds
furrows, ridges, hills, blue mountains;
pebbles gifted with sexual instincts,
sheets calm and clear as sails,
earth of blankets harmonious and good . . .
The bed, you see, is a platform:
it is lifted above everything.
It is, you see, a gigantic vase:
it contains everything.

[3]

I Am the Poet ⧸

I am the poet
and so I have the privilege
of lifting up the bed
and holding it in my hands

As if it were a tinker toy.
I turn it over and over
with wonder as a man who
has just invented something wonderful.

I see people stretching
out their arms in pleas so
gigantic they elude belief.
I glimpse women who can almost hide

Their hands like gloves in the
enlarged pockets of their bellies.
I know men who have been crucified
upon the beds, and even as I hold

My bed, revolving it slowly, a splinter
of what it is, a whisper
of all its silent, brilliant pain
slips, echoing, into me.

Love Is the Builder of the Bed ૨ૐ

Love is the builder of the bed,
she is the original explorer,
she said the bed was like Florida,
because it contained the fountain of youth.

When no one else had courage or foresight,
alone she crossed the plains of the bed;
she trekked and conquered the wild territory,
planted her flag high on the hills of the pillows.

She was like Lewis and Clark,
she wandered far beyond the Mississippi;
she said the bed was a soft, fertile land,
told how it sparkled with dark furrows and promises.

Love is the builder of the bed,
she spanned its rivers with strong, nude bridges,
subdued Indians, planted flowers, and blazed paths
with the skulls of those willing to die for her desire.

Alphabed 🦢

Dayweary? Run to the bed.
Famished for sleep? Eat the bed,
bread. Dive in the pillows, drown
yourself in the rustling billows.
Need a nightschool? Alphabed.
The bed is alpha and omega:
you begin there, you end there.
Fatigued? Put your head on the pillows,
head in the clouds. All for a bed,
for a bit of a bed. Drop to sleep,
dumb with dreams, your belly unfurled
on the deep drum bed. Let your head droop:
after centuries of silence, will the bed yield
and reveal the messages of those
who have slept and long since left?
Tell me a tale of a bed, of a man
and a woman: in the morning, telltale
tracks on the sheets. At night bodies furrow
the bed sod. Bodies freed of minds
thwacked like axes into the bed trunk.
Thirsty? The bed springs will irrigate you.
So don't dread the bed. True, it is a calm,
white tomb. But it's also a mooring, a big
mothering pot to warm you all night long.

The Train Bed 🐦

The bed whistles like a train
and takes off into the night
with its long swaying cargo of sleepy passengers.
The windows are open, the sheets
shine in the moonlight and a seawind smelling
of the grass, the open countries and the cities
that are now left behind rushes in
and lightly plays with the forehead of a girl
who is drowsing. The pillows act as headlights
as dreams rattle and thunder up steep inclines
over dangerous, wooden bridges. The slim
rails along the mattress glisten
solitarily beneath the weight of the darkness.
A few of the passengers snore; others kick
their legs or light cigarettes; the bed does not move,
yet those who are traveling on the bed
first, second or third class, no matter what they are,
who they are, or where they are going,
they are now alone.

Carpenter's Bed ❧

All day I work at planing the bed
and laugh when the white, jagged
shavings fly into my face
like foam; I'm making
the bed smooth and flat for
my beloved; for days now I
have been yearning to lie with her,
but I will not let her come to me
until I have made the bed
as smooth, sleek, and mysterious
as she herself; and so I plane,
sandpaper, rub, and polish it,
soft as grass, smooth as glass;
I mold the mattress like a seastone
until it becomes slender, hollow, dark and opaque,
echoing with desire.
I paint the frame of the bed with
night and instill, infuse, and inject
into it secret, magical words
until the bed ripples and flows
like a lake with the love
of the songs I have created
for it, until the bed dazzles
like a new copper coin in the sun,
and I know my beloved will gleam
like a pitcher on the tablecloth of the sheets;
she will flash and glitter like a sail
on the clear, lacquered waters of the bed.

Spiraled in the Bed with You &

You and I are spiraled
in the bed as lines
into stone, as noise
into shells; the bed
a pale, firm shell of stone
echoes with the converging
forms of our love, we ascend
the bed like riding elevators
to the tops of pyramids;
we descend into it
as birds fall into eggs,
only to climb up again
through the ladders of a narrow
and difficult labyrinth. You streak
the nudity you love, I balance
myself on the bough of your head,
which I caress and kiss as the sea
to smooth, white stones. I have softly
rubbed the triangular pebble
of your sex until it shines like bronze.
Renowned is your trembling
over the plains of the bed
that autumn has drenched with scarlet;
horses have passed by at different speeds,
and it is a pleasure to be trampled with you.

Donkey Bed ⧜

Driven like a donkey the bed,
a hearse, pulls the bodies
of those exhausted by love.

Upon the hills of the tousled sheets
little shepherds bright as stars
have emerged to watch the sad

And ribald procession. The bed
sleek and black, decked with flowery
groans of the conquered, is hauled

Up the steep, wild paths of this
forever unmappable land. Vast
slabs of tangled, weary nudity shine

In the night. The eyes of hidden
animals burn red with curiosity,
the wind piles up deep blue clouds;

The peasant boy whips the donkey
bed, his laughter high, sharp,
burying itself in the hills, the lonely trees.

Rose Bed ❧

O rose of the bed
you are filled with fields,
dream-petals and hollows. You sway
like a white lantern, billow—
a painted cloth hung in the wind.
We grasp you, tightly huddled
beneath your knees as cold children;
you clutch and clothe our trembling
shoulders while the sad bullets
of the night rain down upon us and bruise
the stretched fabric of our flesh.
O rose, rock of the bed,
waves we hurl ourselves again and again
into you as lost, forlorn arrows
released from the taut bow of light
into soft targets of peace night after night,
weary prows crashing against pebbled mattresses.
Like dwarfs, mummies, clowns we seek
to be caught, contained, kept by you
as in the pouch of a kangaroo,
great bright, unfolding rose of the bed.

Cosmic Bed

Born on the bed,
in the old sheet slush,
out of pelagic hips
man heaves back and forth.

No matter what he performs,
he will always return to the bone-
white bed, the old magma mattress
where the sun-womb rotates

Out of which he arose.
Basking in the bed,
borne along by it,
in its rivers and channels

And currents that carry him
into long dream continuums,
his body tills the bed
over which suns have risen and set.

The Bed This Afternoon

The bed this afternoon is filled with clouds.
It is windy. That is why the people
have folded their umbrellas and departed

From the beach of the blue bed. The surface
of the sheets like a lake reflects
the sky, and a young girl comes, stops, and stoops

Above it as if to read her future. Clouds
like parachutes tumbling gently in the bed, the wind
blowing big blue valleys of clarity through the sheets.

Is There a Doctor for the Bed?

You have to examine the inside
of a bed if you want to find out
what it means, what it is all about.
So take a stethoscope: listen

Attentively to how its heart beats,
whether the blood, vitality, enthusiasm
of countless loves has seeped
down into it and irrigated the veins

Or whether only lonely, desperate men
have lain there with their black,
bonebare dreams starving the bed
and wasting it. But poets are doctors

Of experience, so that even if no life
beats in the bed they can still massage
and awaken it to life with their silent,
glowing strength, imagination and love.

Comic Bed ⁀ϡ

Don't say a bed doesn't have
its moments of bad humor! Today
it's coiled up, convoluted and intricate
as a lettuce, proud of the love
that has once filled it, it has extended
itself and possessed the room;
like some enormous serpent, it arches
the sheets into a ball like the back
of a cat; when you and I seek
to approach, it spits, snarls, pretends
we are not good enough! Outside the windows
the leaves are flickering with soft,
bright noise, but what does the bed care?
It's angry. So it sulks. It's arrogant,
so it hides itself like a bird
in the dark, thick bushes of the room.
The glare of its tiny red eyes tells me
that I am in for a long, white night.

Egg Bed 🦢

When the egg
of the bed cracked
open we broke
out of our sleep;
we had been hidden
in the cool, glowing yoke
like pebbles in sand
until one night the stars
plunging into the pool of the sheets
splashed, struggled and made love
with the moon: such
the intensity it warmed, swelled us
out of drowsy, oval yellow; summer nights
chirped like crickets and called us
until impatient with our sleep,
as Venus once out of the sea
we exploded out of the egg of the bed.

Forbidden Bed ತಿ

It ought to be forbidden
to those who have loves
that cannot be fulfilled
to hide their sobs
in the dark cave of our beds,
for those loves will cut
and puncture the rocks like
acetylene torches or whitehot drills.

Bed and Buttocks ⁊❧

Her buttocks swirl like a top
on the pavement of the bed, her buttocks
are flung, they flutter downward dancing in circles
like leaves in the wind; the sand has swelled
up in sudden lumps that resemble her buttocks,
your buttocks are rippling and tracing
patterns on the white earth. She is
sitting up, her legs are sunken like rocks
in the translucent waters of the covers.
She has wrapped her head in the wreath of her arms,
buried herself in the sheath of the sheets
and her buttocks shine like apples a knife has split.
The bed is like a huge hemisphere swept
out and cleansed by the evening wind
to contain the bodies and whirling buttocks of these women.

Bathtub Bed 🦢

Bathing in the bed,
in the soft, profound warmth
are millions of women
who flock to the bed
as birds to telephone wires,
or who throw their bodies like pears
into the cool, silver platter of the bed,
hoping it will cool them;
or who leap into bed
as if it were a bathtub,
and the night will wash over them
as they sink up to their chins
in the foamy sheets,
hoping the morning will find
them clear and fresh.

Shepherd Bed ₰

You have gone
but the shape of you
the traces, paths, and patterns
float on the sky
of the ceiling
beneath which I lie
patient, lonely shepherd
in a tent of sheets
and watch the various constellations
of what you were weave
shuttling back and forth in the darkness
of a room which empty
of you weighs upon me like
a heavy blanket on a summer night.

Fountain Bed 𝄢

Like a fountain the bed
throws up hot, white sparks of joy
into the night, echoing like a piazza
with crowded footfalls of desire.

For once, you are not alone; pillows
surround you like people on steps.
Recklessly you fling yourself into
this rectangular coliseum, the gladiator

Of your heart runs forth, whips
the sword out of his loins and wrestles
with the soft, dark loins of love while
the fountain illuminates the bed with silvery jets.

Triumphant Bed

Look how triumphant the bed!
You have given it many things;
small yet proud of your dreams,
solitude and terrible loves.

Against the dull wall of the room
the bed gleams like a trophy.
You have taught it to leap like a dolphin
beneath the pressure of this exaltation.

It glows like a sunken treasure, you
have encrusted it with your secret,
jeweled world; calm and still as a fish
it lies upon the wharf of what

You left behind you when, a hunter, you crept
through the warm bushes of the day to seize
that shy, fragile, elusive, blonde prey, the prize
who now makes your bed smile and be triumphant.

Blackboard Bed 🐦

Upon the blackboard of the bed
we as children used to write
fantasies and figures of love
with broad, bold gestures of chalk.

We used to ride the bed
into yellow valleys of sleep
as if it were a horse and at night
creeping out beneath the pines

We would rest our heads upon
the soft stones of the pillows;
then, exhausted, the bed would ripple
against us and lull us to sleep like the sea.

Waking early as the dawn we would step
out upon the sheets covered like a field
with the dandelions of a new day:
for a dark, lunatic love rocked in our hearts

And the bed, faithful schooner, was all
we had to take us into secret distant places
where the wind could level the tall
sobs of our desire and softly enisle us in peace.

The Land of Me and the Land of You ⁊❧

You and I lie on the bed
lost in our strange, distant
untouchable love: the bed
freed of its moorings, drifts
away, raft, on the waters of the world.
I try to hold your wrist
which is so thin and afraid of me
it snaps like thread around the button
while love unwinds itself on the spool of me
but you are never there to receive it;
which is why, though I talk endlessly,
I would still need a suspension bridge
if I were ever to walk again
from the land of me into the land of you.

Smokestack Bed 🐦

Telephone wires ought to be strung
over the bed in order
to facilitate communication
between those who are sleeping.

the bed is like a parking lot

Emergency ladders ought to be propped
next to the bed so that he
can follow her when in dreams she
climbs or flies to unassailable heights.

the bed is like a neat cluster
of similar suburban houses

The bed ought to have windows
carved into its walls so that you
could see into the deep dark room
of the other person's insomnia.

the bed is like a freight car on a siding

The bed ought to bob with bright buoys
so that lovers could navigate its
treacherous waters more smoothly and the bed
ought to be honeycombed like a factory

With smokestacks so that all the bitterness
war, sadness, anguish and chaos humanity
gathers and absorbs during the day
could finally be exhaled at night.

Beachball Bed 🐦

You sit astride the bed
like a beachball but it moves
and you roll off.
You watch the tiny swift ripples
that break across the sheets,
you think of a woman you loved:
how she would sit perched
on the beach of the bed
her knees lifted up to her chin
so that her sex would shine warm
as a bronze mollusk on the mattress sand.
You dream of the perfect circles on her chest
and the way she could wind herself
like algae around the rock of you
in the sheet-tossed, surfy sea-bed;
and suddenly you wish the bed were a bottle
so that guzzling it you might soothe
your mind with damp, delicious sleep.

Guitar Bed ₹❧

The guitar on the bed,
the arabesque of the sheets,
the little white fish that hide
in the cove of the pillows
startling you at night;
the sheets unfolded in the morning,
legible as newspapers.
The tapestries of the blankets
which are soft and simple, of black
and white design, with animals
rushing across them.
The sill of the bed
upon which you sit when you are bored;
then you look through the windows
at cool, bright landscapes of dreams.
The dark flute of your love
which you pipe only
when you crouch between her thighs.
The guitar of her loins,
the ballroom of the bed,
the bed which is perpetual dance;
the remembrances of her body which leapt
like a porpoise in and out of the sheets . . .
And now the yellow seeds that sometimes soar
up from the loins of the bed guitar,
notes of nostalgia shining in the air.

Sleeping Woman Bed ॐ

The woman sleeps. She
has one huge breast
that glows like a lamp.
She dreams, massive
and indolent on the iceberg
of the bed. Black and white
penguins strut about her.
She dreams of trolleycars
and streetlamps. The bed,
dazzling and warm, drifts
through the water.
Her buttocks are so
open and so split
they resemble halved
pears; and the bed
wanders away in the
water like the
blue sky
because it too
has started to dream
just looking
at them.

Ache Bed 🦢

This bed is blistered,
too many women have cursed it;
it is scorned, solitary and outcast
for young girls have fled it in terror.
It is tortured and dumb
because men of great love
have lain upon it alone;
it is bloody and dark because
soldiers gashed and torn by chaos,
war, and darkness have tried
to find some peace upon it at last.
It is bandaged and burned
because the poor have stabbed it,
their desperation having no other target;
and the rich have tossed it like a log
into the little bonfires of their lust.
The bed too has looked for tenderness,
for love and dreams soft as bread in the night;
but it has too often been hurled
like a carton of rags or dead fish
into the street. O it has been gutted,
its ribs broken, slashed, flung out, because
the bed has glimpsed no harmony,
no point of possible junction between
the mind the sleepers live in
and the world in which they must walk.
Ah the ache of this bed!

Cracked Bed 🦢

Then we made love.
I lay on top of you,
spinning like a top
on the floor of your flesh.

Clinging to you like a sheet
on a sweltering summer night.
The heat generated
by our churning bodies

Smirched the windows!
My hips no longer mine.
Upon the bed everything unified
except the outcast pillow.

Thrusting your legs around me,
you squeezed. I slipped
in and out of you
like a beachball. Your buttocks

Felt so large they made
me live twice. Your fervencies
shrunk the bed like
a newly laundered shirt.

Now it's over, your sex
glued upon you, damp red leaf.
You flattened on the bed
as if struck by an automobile.

So you are neighboring
on chaos and death;
the lonely bed gleaming,
cracked at the seams.

Newspaper Bed ॐ

There are many things that resemble a bed
to which a bed can be compared
but most of all a newspaper resembles a bed:
can you guess why? Because a bed
is always spread open, it splits
itself like an apple or the thighs of a woman
and offers itself to whoever asks of it. It
is always there, always present, in
the morning, in the evening, you can find
it as easily as a newspaper, it is not
secret, difficult or private, it is open
exposed, unfurled like a flag, nude.
You can squint at it, you can drowse before
the pages of the sheets, you can perambulate
it with your eyes or take a long walk
within it, you can even die within it.
And many things have seeped into it, not only
what is 'fit to print,' but like a lithograph
stone it has been stamped
with all the legends, dreams, memories of mankind;
it is a kind of fossil upon which
have been imprinted all the possible moods,
moments, gestures, desires, and configurations of love;
and as an ordinary daily newspaper collects
and reports everything, the crime and the lust
and love, so a bed though it absorbs,
though it takes and gives, each morning is always

[33]

fresh, is forever being made up, recomposed
and edited anew, the contents of an old story
endlessly transcribed and permutated, one history
of your life written in tiny detail on the scroll
of the bed while the newspaper, parallel, captures
the other, your waking life: thus the bed becomes
the newspaper of sleep and dreams the headlines
which influence you and finally force you to act.
And so the ceaseless variation of the same theme
continues and the bed, white petal of paper
cool, thin slab of sheets, stands before you,
offered, shining and cool, a fountain
in a public square and you have only to sit
on a green park bench, prop it on your knees, unfold
and read it to know all
the information, glory, sadness and love of the world.

Raging Bed

Pinch the bed!
Its thighs! Squeeze dreams
out of it as paint out of tubes,
juice out of oranges!
Punch the bed!
Make it sway back and forth
before you like the head of a boxer.
Indent, carve and deepen the bed,
make it harsh, rugged as a ravine,
crate it, stomp it!
Grind yourself into it like sand;
chalk, scrawl or slash the fury
and despair of yourself upon it.
Drill it! Saw it! Rasp it!
Stamp it as print a page
with minute holes, hollows, sweeping curves
until it thunders like a trumpet with torment!
Rip it roughly with your fingers,
tear the sheets like sails!
Take a spade and dig a grave
of hopeless calm for yourself within it;
stake it out and drench it with the red-
painted slabs of your loss.
Puncture it like a balloon!
Spark, illumine and burn it,
this solitary plank of a bed

packed with emptiness, pocked
with craters, the pillows crushed
like raw, soggy hamburgers;
into which, now, you rage.

Lonely Woman Bed ⅋

How alone she lies, the young woman,
clutching her pillow as if it were
a cradle and she yearning
to be buried within it.
She sleeps calmly
in the garden of the bed, now and then
an apple thuds against the earth
of the sheets. How soft and tender
her body, it casts large shadows
which also do not belong to her.
The grass grown high as flutes
pipes secret litanies around her.
Her hands jammed into the muffler
of her neck, she lies on her loins;
her crossed legs shape and instruct
the sad, yielding form of her buttocks
in such a way that they shoot off sparks
of an incredible. nearness, gentleness and pain.

Quiet Shell Bed ॐ

The bed is a shell and we
live within it, long
slender waves of love have washed
against our bodies filling them

With an ancestral pain. The bed
an island, we stranded upon it,
airplanes flashing with red lights
fly above us in the night.

We convene within the forum
of the bed, it is a monument
built next to the rocks and the sea,
illuminated prison of love

Pyramid or prism through which we
in sleep are refracted while all
the shrapnel the day, soldier, has shot
into us is softened, calmed and stilled.

Autumn Bed 𓅯

In the autumn the leaves
of limbs are scattered
over the wide scarlet
plains of the bed,
the sheets dark yellow, fragrant
like an old garden.
In the summer
bed was white, the love
of everything reflected upon
the surface as sycamores in water.
Now jackdaws screech from the fenceposts
of the bed and middle-aged women
blonde and calm as cows, graze
amid the memories of what they were
or what they might have been.

Rain Pain Bed &

The bed tonight dark with rain,
I have covered you with
the sheets of my pain.

We sleep separately
our bodies forming
separate, dark pools of clarity.

Sleepy, you move your hands over
and wade a little
through the shallows and shadows of me.

But the bed gleams
like a desolate plain,
the bed tonight dark with rain

Because I have covered you with
the shadows
and sheets of my pain.

Pregnant Woman Bed ३⋟

I salute you,
the child that is in you;
as you step up to the door
of the bed, your belly-
laden bough hanging from you,
should I turn you and your burden away?
But lying on my back I stretch
out my left arm in an effort
to welcome you, remembering how you
once let me touch and turn
the silver doorknob of your loins,
how transparent and porous you were!
Tonight something else is pressing out against
the curving, warm walls of your stomach,
a strange light is shining upon us,
all my sadness is hidden in my ribs,
and what you are about to give
is more than what I ever could put into you.
A child should come and gently
tug the balloon of your belly and pull
you into the sky. The bed too
is more yours than mine and now you walk
into it and the dark complicity of the sheets,
as a woman heavy with promise strides
into the mansion that has been promised her.

3:15 A.M. 🦢

I am sleeping. It is
a summer night. The sheets
cling to the numb stilts
of my legs like sediment.
You can't sleep. It's 3:15 A.M.
One of my arms is buried
beneath the mound of the pillow,
the other is thrown
rather casually across it.
Sleep seems to have shrunken my head,
the skin's stretched tight
across my chest and all my ribs
are shining vaguely
like fishscales. You lean back
on the edge of the bed. Your body
looks dark and heavy. I can't see
your face. It's as if
you were sitting at the prow
of the bed waiting for it to move,
but it doesn't. And it's 3:15 A.M.

Palimpsest Bed ᙖ

Palimpsest,
the bed fades.

How many different impressions of life
written upon it since time began?

The sheets like surfboards
have glided and plunged

Up and down how many times,
and how many times has the thread

Of a man's sex been wound into
the spool of a woman's loins?

What number of bodies swept up
at random upon it have crowded

It as pebbles a beach? Is the bed
a moviescreen across which the faces of love

Have unfolded? A shewolf, mankind sucking
the teat pillows? A dreamtight compartment,

Skyscraper of sleep? A lofty, windplucked
plateau where bodies crash like meteorites?

Yet how safely you sleep, solitude wrapped
around you like a coat of chainmail.

The Bed, the Desert Spaces, and You ⪼

Unroll your body like a flag
across the bed.
Then let the wind
which roams in from the sea
through the windows blow and billow you.

Pretend you are hiding, hunched
up beneath the pillow dunes.
Because you are afraid of the wind,
you crouch squatting,
molded like clay into a ball

Upon the contours of the bed,
craters, the sudden ravines.
As a rabbit you seek to burrow
a hole into the handpacked,
hardly textured sand of the sheets,

But the wind whirls you about
the clean, scooped out curves of the bed
like a marble, and you cower
your fear making you wrap yourself,
a vine, about the body of whoever

Is near to you. And it is not the wind
that troubles you so much as
the desert spaces that are its mother.

Candelabra Bed ⁊

Candelabra of the bed
holding you up,
containing your soft, tender warmth;
upon which during the night
like a candle lit by love
you burn and sputter
as the cantaloupe of your haunches
moistens the sheets.
You turn your back to him,
shutting out the universe;
your several dreams branch
out on the candelabra of the bed.
How lightly the burden
of your body floats
on the dilapidated mattress.
But you are not alone:
even sailors sleep in beds.
The bed holds the weary, the lost
like a home that understands all languages.
Hopes, desires savage as January
light drowse slowly on the massive pillow,
where you have pressed your tender skull,
hungry for sleep; while the old bed,
candelabra, carries you forward nobly
as the carriages in Central Park
toward the shy, blue-fingered morning.

Bowl Bed &

So here you are, limp again
crumpled on the bed
like a piece of paper,
exhausted, limp, dead.
Bed-dead. And hot. The sheets
so damp pressed against you.
"Do you know what time it is?"
"Must be about five-o'-clock."
"Why don't you pull the shades?
All that sun." "O.K." It's cooler
now, blankets of shadows
reach up to your hips.
You're so beautiful,
you make me jealous of sharing
you with the bed into which
you're molded as the bodies
of bathers into sand. Too bad
refrigerated beds didn't exist
so that after making love
you wouldn't suffer so much
from the heat sparked in the flesh.
Perhaps I can cool you with my hands,
my hands like water moving over you
so lightly and softly. O I could dream . . .
In the late afternoon we lie floating
on the wide linen pond like lily pads.

Then darkness deepens the bed, emptying
it of all but ourselves.
Invisible, shielded from the wind
we repose in the bowl bed.

Sleepwalker ह्•

Sleepwalker, you,
why do you persist
in making your legs
gallop across the sheets like ponies?

The bed is so parched
from lack of the sleep
you could not give it,
cracked as soil after months of no rain.

Like a target you are riddled
with the bullets of your sleeplessness;
You ought to sit upright and look
at what is happening to you

Instead of squashing your head
like a pumpkin in the pillow
until the pillow is hammered
around your skull like a horseshoe.

Wildlife Refuge Bed ॷ

As the sky is like a blue pad
upon which the fingerprints of birds
are pressed, so we draw patterns
on the bed.
The sheets are coiled,
the linen is whorled;
our bodies late in love like leaves
have turned, but you are still
stretched out before me as shadows
on a summer lawn. O we would need
a bulldozer to clear away the debris
of our love from the streets
of the sheets. The folds in your flesh
are equal to the folded blankets.
Ah my pale straw wisp, the bed
is the only barn we have left
in which weary, bloodstitched animals
we can find refuge and peace.

All Bed ⁊❧

All seeps into it.
Overflowing with life,
the bed is everywhere,
vibrant with departed love.

Roll in the taut, white Eden where
dreams are still deep and bright;
hide like a cluster of snow
in the curving hollows of the sheets.

Hushed, sleep holds the stage.
Forget the terrors of our age.
Love, which is gust, will efface
any blur, shrieks, or traces of you.

The flesh has tattooed no stories
on the skin of the sheets, and the bed
is no daguerrotype. But when half-asleep
in the late afternoon you lie

Derailed on the bed, rattling and rumbling
like a train will the night appear
to haul you back to all the tiny
blinking stations of your childhood.

Upon the Bed Sands 🦢

Everyone must know how
after making love
the bed becomes so fragmented
you have to pick it up and put
it back together again like the pieces
of a jigsaw puzzle,
and you yourself become so small
you feel about like a cowskull or pebble
lying there upon the wide, expanded
plains or sands of the bed.

Buried Treasure Bed ૐ

The bed so ruffled,
with our hands have we dug
for treasures in the white
and dark soil of the sheets?

Only when sleep's bow has released us
can night, red arrow of sap, flow.
O how many relics are buried
in the pillow? Bed, secret museum

where under the ground of the blankets
flesh loved too much conceals itself.
The bed is mild and drowsy tonight,
so I light you like a kerosene lamp;

and this glow begins to bring
the counterpanes to life: the late afternoon
sun shines, and I tremble, straining
to telescope 2000 years of life, love and pain.

Bed for a Majestic Woman 🦢

I want to sketch a woman on a bed,
show her within the frame of a bed,
and what the various possibilities are
for her to be there.
Her breasts dangle from her
like conical flashlights
and illuminate the sheets
as the headlights of an auto on a country road
at night do to the trees.
Her loins like white paper
float almost a rectangle within the larger
more concrete rectangle of the bed;
in the middle of the page of her loins
someone, curious, bored or naughty schoolboy?
has scrawled a huge V, and that V
complicates the bed, adds to it like a tributary
something extremely difficult and dark, an arabesque
of ferns, complex labyrinth that might explode
with pain and depth and warmth, and it makes
of the bed a sort of sponge, or something sweet
damp and soft capable of absorbing you
and drenching up all the nervousness
of your lonely sorrow.
The hips of the woman can swivel
and give to the bed a fresh
and interesting mobility and lightness.
If you have ever seen a bed

anchored in a room alone
you will know what a heavy,
ponderous and rusty thing it is;
which is why a woman is necessary to a bed
as water is necessary to soil,
to feed, moisten and keep it vital and alive.
Hopefully the woman's navel will be large
enough to blaze like a solar cymbal
in the night of the bed.
If she is a true woman,
she will sketch herself endlessly upon the stretched
canvas of the sheets, and the bed will be
continually modified, amplified and varied
by the shadows, movements, intonations,
nuances, depths and meaning
of her painterly, majestic presence.

Holiday Bed 🦢

The bed is white
as a holiday, to the workers
it shines like Casablanca
or Nice, it is
a farm, nudity
the eternal crop, it
can be a village, uniting
our terrible separateness in
some primitive order. O bed,
couch, melody, green
and blue hammock
of days, you permit
us to grow green
again within you
when the world has made
us brown; to those starved,
broken, uprooted, scattered
like cinders you unfold
yourself, azure banner
of the bed in the sky
of our hearts; calm,
peaceful as grain, but
how rugged, not combustible,
so that even if the fires
of past tortures or loves
streak and splay your dreams,
bed will not burn like a barn.

So listen to the melody
that springs like the water
of days from the
green and white meadows
of the bed, where every night,
as in a large, simple market, we
go shopping for the royal, substantial
bread, meat, the essential fish
the day has somehow failed to give us.

Saluting the Bed 🐎

Overshadowed
   by the leaves
      of the bodies of love;

Illuminated stage
   where a woman
      endlessly interprets her nudity;

Map of contours,
   swell of linen
      dampened by waves of love;

Flat, open grove
   of tranquillity and peace,
      public square where the loins

I loved are impressed and still
   sometimes are arched, into
      which I so often ramified myself;

I salute you, bed.

Atlas Bed 🦢

This drowsy bed
sprinkled with your body,
garden suspended
in the space of the room,
planet revolving
in the wide night of our love,
ah! The silver strata of the sheets
in which our hands dive and dig,
creating our own suns and moons
for all time! Don't break the bed,
rather let the darkness be converted
by the twin beacons of your breasts
and the lighthouse of your loins,
turning slowly round and round.
O illumined night of sheets and stars!
And like a long, cool surf, mystery
whispering up and down within it.
Enisled, whorled, strong
the nearly empty bed stands
there like Atlas holding up
the sky with our nearly absent love.

Joyous Jug Bed

On the table of the bed
we are like jugs:
we dance on the linen,
but unlike most people
we never pour ourselves out;
our happiness lies
in our calmness, coolness and restraint.
Our bodies are jugs,
we waltz at night
on the tablecloth of the bed;
we caress with our water
the cheek of the bed,
and we dream
of the clouds of your hips,
sweet, raw milk of your hips
spilled and flowing across
the table of the bed where we,
joyous jugs, dance.

Hugging the Pillow ᘒ

You hug the pillow
as if it were a raft
and you were floating downstream
and about to be lost.

Lying on your side you squeeze
it between your knees as if
it were the only love you
had left, or as if you

Had never loved at all.
You embrace the pillow with such
frenzy and wildhaired desperation
that one might take you for a child.

You cling to it exactly
as a frightened child clings
to and rides with his knees upon
the fantastic locomotive of his dreams.

Barber Bed

Bed, barber
will cut
hair of dreams
if too long for life.

Bed, umbrella
will shelter
will cool
if sun too hot.

Bed, deep dark garage
will hold you
if place cannot be found
in parking lot of world.

Hill Bed 🦢

The bed is a hill.
All night long alone you labor in your sleep
and like Sisyphus try to tote the burden
of she who is not with you
to the top.
Like a cow you graze on the slopes
of the sheets, the pain
of her absence tinkling in your ear.
All you desire is to rest,
to make the bed into something your own,
friendly and warm instead of alien and hostile.
How can you reconcile the forces that lurk
beneath the mound of the blankets
which collapse around your knees
like popped balloons? As you sleep your mind
climbs toward the summit of a pale, smooth love
without mornings or farewells,
and the ceiling is flooded with constellations
which are the shadows of your dream.
Everything you did or have not done
returns to haunt you now,
as you lie on the bitter bedrock,
on this hollow tindrum of a mattress.
The pillows make love by themselves.
The sheets reflect the night like silver lakes.

Boat Bed

Slapping and sloshing
against the borders of the bed
like boats against the wharves
of the bay are our bodies
which swell like rubber dirigibles
with the ballooning air of love
until the sheetsea begins to get noisy
and crashes around our hips,
boom! So we pound each other
and into the bed spinning like a whirlpool
topsy-turvy! upside down! are we sucked
and almost drowned in the miserable
arms of each other! Screwed
to the careening raft
of the bed! Crucified!
Our thighs swept away by the undertow
of love's sweet bitter purple foam
which you spew out!
O baby! Don't fall off the bed
as Christopher Columbus might
have fallen off the earth
if it had been flat!
Meanwhile the cool moon gleams
through the window upon the granite
cracks of this lunar, love-blasted bed
where we ache exhausted, blowing
our own moons out of our mouths.

When Will the Bed Awake? &

Someone has stepped all over us.
They have impressed their feet
upon my stomach and your back.

Our nudities have been trampled so much
that we have been separated;
the rinds of our bodies have been cast

Away from the damp, glowing globe
of our love. Now you sleep, your head
has created a dark dent in the pillow.

I can no longer see your hair or your neck.
My own head wallows in the swamp
of my pillow; my navel gapes

Open, a crater; my sex squeezed
and rubbed between my legs like a sharp
pebble into sand. I am dreaming of when

You will wake up and thinking of the
thousands of ancestors who have traversed us,
leaving footprints. When will the bed awake?

Battlefield Bed ⦵

My sex drips
like a fishing pole
between my legs,
and I lean toward you

Trying to talk. You
are bowed and submissive
as a nun, and the sheets
drape the plum

Of your nudity like
a bishop's robe. A
gaunt man, I am nailed
to the plank of the bed;

Behind me glows the recent
battlefield. I feel more twisted
and torn than my face, I labor
toward you, but you can't answer.

Cliff Bed 🦆

You are crushed
within the burlap texture of the bed,
your hips blotted
in a white desert of sheets.

You nestled
in the shrubbery of sheets,
accumulations of darkness around you,
your knees puffed up.

Then a fear shakes you,
the blankets collapse like balloons.
Bent above you, my body
clusters together like iron filings

Before a magnet. But you rise,
squat on the bed as if perched
on a cliff, hugging
yourself, indifferent, solitary.

Revelation Bed ⪜

Suddenly the tent
arched above the bed was ripped
away and we were exposed,
our vulnerable bodies perched
upright on the massacred sheets!
The whole bed shone
as if it had just gulped down the dawn,
and the light was drained
up into you until your breasts
glowed like a double Tour Eiffel;
and as an idea is transformed by art,
so your hair into a rivulet, a massive
inundation of shadow. I felt
as if we were sitting on a beach
and the beach had been stripped
of its sand and made nude.
High upon the ceiling our shadows
watched and imitated us, but I shoved
the humble, painful whisper of my head
into the harbor of your shoulders.
Your body curved up to me beneath
hands of brightness, spreading the cry
of an intimacy so enormous that I tottered.
Yet you just lay, lowered your head and waited;
and miles away from us the pillows were scattered,
swept up upon the bed like early seaweed.

[68]

Young Girl Alone 🐚

Tonight, alone, you
are wrapped like a mummy
on the bare, abandoned bed.

Someone who is gone
has molded you like dough
into the long, dense forms of pain.

Yet you have hurled
aside the cry of the sheets,
they rot like rubbish on the side

Roads of the bed. The pillow
behind you shines vacant
as the throne of an assassinated king.

Mute, invisible, faceless,
smooth, effaced, like a loaf
of sand, you, a young girl

Now lie wrapped uniquely
in the textures, the cold
empty blankets of your own sorrow.

Sad Bed

The bed is sad as a creature in grief,
it is a box with the corpses of o
so many loves locked inside it.
And I know the misery of the lonely sheets,
the dolor of shadowy, immobile pillows,
the stripped desolation of the mattress,
the cry of a newspaper, stranded, unfolded
on the bed in the stale light of late morning;
womanly bodies so saturated with love
they reek like winestaves, the desperate
duplication night after night of dreams,
limbs, faces and styles of love. I have seen
charwomen with brooms sweeping away the dust,
collection of innumerable tedium, from the floor
of the bed; I know that beds can be chopped
by swiftly striking hands of passion into
slender, white slices of softness; but above all
the bed is a coliseum of blood and sobs,
it has the inexorable sadness of a summer night
in mid-August. Soon breezes will make,
as always, the sheets grow cooler
and death will glaze the flesh of the bed
with a new and yet finer coat of paleness.

Seem to steal from Roethke.

Good-bye Bed

On a deserted bed
where everything has burned,
bodies consumed like logs,
which even the flame has abandoned
so that only white ashes are left.
On a bare, blank bed
old as a medieval city,
washed by the light and the wind,
a bed once filled with sleepers
as market street in morning with walkers,
a bed achingly sweet to remember,
from which no woman again will rise,
where at night there will be no more fire or laughter,
a tender bed, deep, muddy with memories,
undone, undoing like the spring,
to which I must now return to say good-bye.

Fireworks Bed 🐦

Night! The wind driving sand across the bed,
the bed like a peasant cart rocking
on the ruts of sleep. I a man
with a face cracked like glass hold a whip
and drive the donkey bed into dark lands
that glow with grain. Sheets rustle like fields,
and I think of the inundation of your thighs,
the clear, natural crack between them,
hair which flows and melts in the shadowy
textures of the sheets while breasts wage
silent battles with the pillows. I remember
your large belly ajar: open house,
will it welcome me again when I
grow tired of this wandering?

          Some day clouds will sail
with the blimp of your belly across the sky
of the bed, accompanying it as dolphins
a boat in southern seas; as a coconut
from palm tree flesh a lazy blonde, beautiful
child I hope will fall from you.

          And the bed shepherd
safely hidden in mattress valleys, thrusting
forth his flute, lance, between the bush pillows . . .

But the bed, petal-shaped, so small my thumb
could mold it as, lily pad, it floats
through the pond-room, how I desire to stamp
my body's fingerprint upon it. You
and I for so many nights yoked to the blue
plough of love have crossed and zigzagged
it with furrows, the multiple lines of passion
until, soft flower of clay, it has captured
our sadness, rage and despair; yet has such
a fragile stem, touch with your fingers and watch
it crumble.

> let's bicycle around the bed
> or take a kayak ride down sleep

> > Bed, watering hole
> > where men like wild horses
> > stampede in the evening
> > to drink their pleasures;
> > Bed, waterfall
> > down which a man can cascade
> > bobbing in the barrel
> > of a belly of a woman.

> or walk the busy boulevards of dreams

Have you wounds? The sheets will bandage them.
Only wrap yourself on the spool of sleep and let
Chinese lanterns project dreams on the ceiling:
images of yourself, child, bouncing up
and down on the mattress trampoline . . . But wave,
you roll over me, a sudden undertow of sleep
takes me off my feet; but what a sparse
noble sea you are, your silent, strong
clarity counterweight to my fragility
and pain.

>Think of all the reflections
>that have been poured into the bed
>like light onto pavements,
>and how many bodies have stooped
>above that smooth, white, oblong shape,
>having refused to slam the doors
>on desire and seeking to quench
>themselves like young blue horses
>in the stream of the sheets.

Now your hips are extended into the air
above the bed like coat hangers from
which, loosely, the tattered shirt
of your flesh drips. Stiff as slingshot forks
your legs are jerked apart, and your soul:
the long eroded yet still jagged pebble you yearn
to have sprung out of you into the sky.

Nothing but the sobs of your desire have gouged
out the pillow so that it looks like a horseshoe
crammed and lost in which your head now whirls.

Remarkable how the bed, bulb, glows
when you press your lips against her;
or, electric guitar, throbs, expands
and is filled with this wonderful
trembling when you enfold her.

Afterward: hunched over the same spot
of the bed, roughly the center,
looking for something we peer down,
our faces fixed together, perhaps the
surface of the bed is only a veil, simple
crust of earth beneath which floats that
magical world we long for, at any rate looking
together creates a sense of communion; it's after
midnight, how pleasant it is being hunched over
shoulder to bare shoulder in the midst of the darkness.

Then you fall asleep:

you in your sleep are an old locomotive,
you hug the rails of the bed
around sharp, shiny curves; ponies
graze beside you in the dark
pastures of the room, the paths
of trees cover mountains, and they hunch
over you like spies; you love the way
the bed quivers beneath the rocking
impulse of your railroad motion while smoke
packed tightly together as shrubs billows
out of the smokestack of your dreams.

And my sex is a cue and I stroke
the blue billiard ball of your body across
the pale, rippled velvet of the sheets.

Although the valley of the bed was filled
with cries, linen cooled those murdered by love.
But women also have been caught like insects
in the white gigantic web of the bed.
For me the bed has been a wall against which
blindfolded, I have been placed countless times
and shot by the girl I loved.

But your love
so brilliant makes the bed shine
like aluminum, your love extensive
so much so that now all the beds
you have ever slept in stand up
like soldiers in a row and shine
like aluminum.

We are lying in the grove
of the bed, I am trying to dig
a grave in your hips
with the spade of my sex
and then bury myself within it—

the sheets pulled around us like pelts.

But watch out: the mattress, big-game trap
has its steel springs coiled back ready
to snap the moment you try to taste the body-
bait of that wild, treacherous woman you adore.

She lies clutching her heart.
The empty pillow! A spotlight
illumines her. She is trying to save
herself, but absence has a way
of prolonging itself, the very space
it creates becoming necessary to you.
Now she needs that emptiness, as much
as she rebels against it and twists
her face away, as if not to look.

As for us, we were shipwrecked in the room. The
vessel of our love couldn't carry us any farther.
But finding an island, we clung to it: how surprised
we were when the sheets swelled up and the bed
started to sail, bearing us to another port of which
you were the nude admiral!

These things were not for him: he slept, his
jaw unshaven; the yellow lamp, serpent, quivers
over the headboard; the blankets reeking with stale
life; his nose blotted against the inkpad of his
hands; his limbs awry as weeds; behind him, through
the open window, the sun has just risen, calm,
hollow circle . . .

Sun on the bed,
bulb above the bed,
high noon of the bed,
light of the sheets,
shadow of her body;
the house of her loins
awakes to greet the sun
streaming far above
the bluffs of the bed;
blankets, wet foliage
cool depth, dark waters
and sheets, hillsides
where, shepherd, she still
pastures her warm dream goats.

Make love until, exhausted, we sprawl
like wine bottles that have waltzed all night
upon the gleaming table, floor, of the bed.

It is autumn:
the old brown leaves of the sheets
rustle in the ravine of the bed.
The brown rain of our love
flutters slowly down the gutter of the bed.
How crisp, cold, clear, dry and ancient I feel today!
I wish the bed were a lake
so that all the sorrows, guilt and horrors of myself
might be pumped out of me while I sleep,
emptied, released and hidden within it.

Then the wind came, broom, sweeping the bed,
flattening it, washing out of it the darkness
and the dust, making it hard, white, immaculate
as desert sand, without a ripple or ruffle;
but you loll at the window looking at it
and say, 'How different it is!'
Glancing at you, the nude, bare, desolate
plains of your flesh, I wonder if the wind
has not swept you too?

Now slabs cover the bed,
craters, gullies and fissures
as deep and wide as the one
I once knew between your thighs.
The bed is deserted.
The passions of many men have left
the blankets twisted like lava.
Rift, jagged, the bed glows
with the pride of its conquered solitude.